Faith over Fear

Faith over Fear

Denise Montgomery
by 'Deep Works'
Teaching and Healing
Ministry

2 Timothy 1:7
For God hath NOT GIVEN us the spirit of fear; but of power, and of love and of a sound mind

CONTENTS

INTRODUCTION	
FAITH OVER FEAR	1
HOW FEAR GOT A HOLD OF ME	5
FALSE EVIDENCE APPEARING REAL	15
ABUSED BY MY FATHER	19
LIVING WITH FEAR	27
WHEN MY BODY BROKE DOWN	41
THEN I MET JESUS	47
FREEDOM FROM FEAR	57
RENEWING OF MY MIND	65
MINDLESSNESS	77
WHAT I FEARED CAME UPON ME	83
THERE'S POWER IN THE WORD	87
STRONGHOLDS	103

INTRODUCTION

I decided to write this book to share part of my life's journey, my story on how I overcame fear with faith. This book shares some of my testimony of how broken I was, and how fear had a hold of me, ensnaring me and was controlling how I lived my life, and today I am able to testify that I am free from the spirit of fear.

I was broken, I had deep wounds, deep wounds from my past that were not healing. As I grew older those wounds were still very real to me and were still very raw. The memories from my past, I could relive in my mind more than 25-30 years later, feeling those same emotions I felt back then. That replay was very real, playing out in my mind regularly.

Many people come from different backgrounds, some come from a loving home, some from broken homes, some from abusive backgrounds. I am one that has come from an abusive background and a broken home.

My heart's desire is that as you read this book that you would see that you are not alone, that someone cares, someone loves you, that you can find freedom from torment and fear and from your past hurts.

No matter what you have been through in life, there is a way of escape. You don't have to let what you have lived through in your past become your future or let it be who you are.

YOU DON'T HAVE TO LET WHAT YOU LIVED THROUGH IN YOUR PAST BECOME YOUR FUTURE OR LET IT BE WHO YOU ARE!

For me, torment and fear came into my life around the age of 11-13 years old, to my recollection.

I was woken out of my sleep to find my father touching me. I pretended to sleep, keeping my eyes closed. When he had left I remember getting up and putting on 3-4 layers of night dresses, one on top of the other. I cried quietly curled up in a ball. I did not sleep that night. From that night onwards I was changed. My childhood innocence was taken and destroyed by what my father had done. Back in those days I was sent out of the room if any adult material came onto the television, so as a child I was shielded from anything sexual or graphic. I was still very naive.

Life changed for me from that night, I changed from a care free child to a child who was burdened, frightened, broken, betrayed and ashamed. Hiding a dark secret I dared not speak of. I was told by my father, that if I spoke of what he was doing, it would be my fault that the family would break up.

To my recollection the abuse continued until I was around 15-16 years old. I was in my last year or last couple of years at high school.

This was when I spoke out. I had broken down in front of a friend and shared with her what had been going on. With my friend's encouragement, I shared what had been happening with my mother, by writing her a note telling her that my father was "a dirty old man". It was a very simple note that I pushed into her hand before I went out for the evening with some friends, stressing to her not to let my father see it.

I thank God that my mother believed me. Action was taken and my father was later sentenced to some time in prison.

My father may have done a few years in prison, but my prison sentence continued, I did not have a 'get out of jail card' that I knew of at that time. I was very bitter and angry at my father for what he had done to me. I blamed him for who I was and what I had become. I felt I was dirty, broken, damaged goods and he was responsible.

I tried counselling over the years and some of it did help me have some sort of a life, to function, but I was not free. I still relived the nightmares of my past. I still felt damaged, unlovable and broken.

My 'get out of jail' card came when I gave my life to the Lord Jesus Christ. He was the one that was able to set me free, free from torment and fear. No-one other than Jesus could do the deep work that needed to be done deep inside of me.

Man cannot see all that is within you, only God can see this. He sees the heart, He knows your thoughts, He sees your tears when you think no-one else is looking.

What I have learned is that when I was in torment with the pain of my past, my body was also in dis-ease. I had numerous infections, bleeding in my urine, palpitations etc. These, I believe, came because of the emotional distress my body was in.

There is freedom and healing that comes from the Lord Jesus Christ. He is the only one that can do the deep work in you. Together you can overcome and have victory in your life. He is the one who heals the broken hearted and is the lifter of your head.

I pray that this book is a blessing to those who read it and that you will find freedom from fear through the Word of the Lord and my testimony.

Denise

CHAPTER ONE

FAITH OVER FEAR

The scripture I will start with is:-

For God hath NOT GIVEN us the spirit of fear; but of power, and of love and of a sound mind.
2 Timothy 1:7

We all can experience a "fight or flight" response to something that causes us to be afraid, for example, when someone jumps out on you and you jump and your heart starts to pound because you were not expecting it. This is quite normal. This response is an automatic physiological reaction to an event that is perceived as stressful or frightening. This prepares the body to fight or flee. It's known as the "fight or flight" response.

This is not the same as a spirit of fear. A spirit is a being. You can read in the Word of God, Jesus addressed them, He spoke directly to them and commanded them to leave. (Matthew 8:16, Mark 1:34, Mark 5:8, Luke 4:35, Luke 11:14)

When dealing with a spirit of fear it is as if he gets into your head. You dialogue with him. You believe the lies. The spirit of fear wants to control your life to keep you in bondage. He wants you to believe that bad things will happen or happen to people you love.

When I would go for a walk in a forest park I would see bad things happening, like a branch whacking me on the face or stumbling on a stone and falling, hurting myself. This was continual, I would have to stop myself from reacting to what I was seeing. These images made me very cautious when I was out somewhere. They were never real. What they were was FEAR -

False **E**vidence **A**ppearing **R**eal.

The spirit of fear is torment, is death, is destruction. It steals your peace! It is not from God but from the devil!

The thief cometh not, but for to steal, and to kill, and to destroy: I am come that they might have life, and that they might have it more abundantly.
*** John 10:10***

CHAPTER TWO

HOW FEAR GOT A HOLD OF ME!

I wanted to share my testimony on this subject, not just to share what I have been through but for you to grab a hold of this scripture that fear is not of God, that it's NOT something that He wants you to live with or be tormented by.

As I thought about my life, the times that I was so fearful and overcome by anxiety these are the words that came to my mind. These are what I was feeling and what I was experiencing in my body. This was very real, I lived in that world described by the words below:-

- TORMENT
- SLEEPLESSNESS
- STRESS
- HEAVINESS
- SELFISHNESS
- DEPRESSION
- IRRATIONAL THOUGHTS
- WEARINESS
- LONELINESS
- SELF PITY
- I CAN'T - FEARFUL
- NEGATIVITY
- OVERREACTION
- ISOLATION
- SHAME
- PROCRASTINATION
- FRUSTRATION
- HOPELESSNESS
- DESPAIR

SUICIDAL THOUGHTS

OVERWHELMED

AT BREAKING POINT

DARKNESS

ANGER

NO WAY OF ESCAPE - TRAPPED

BENT OVER

BURDENED

BROKEN

CURSED

WEAKNESS

SOURNESS

IN A DARK HOLE

IMPRISONED

FEELING THAT I CAN'T COPE

HATING LIFE

DEATH

HELD CAPTIVE BY THOUGHTS

ENSNARED

REJECTION
UNFORGIVENESS
BITTERNESS

Bodily reactions:-
LACK OF ENERGY
LOSS OF CONTROL OVER BODY - FROZEN IN FEAR
PANIC ATTACKS
SWEATING
DIARRHOEA
VOMITING
TEARS
PUPUTATIONS
INFECTIONS
TENSION
SICKNESS
HEADACHES

When I think about my life now, my life with Jesus, now knowing Him close to 13 years these are the words that come to my mind and what I can and do experience in my everyday life.

PEACE
JOY
CALMNESS
REST
LOVED
COMPASSION
WISDOM
OVERCOMER
SECURITY
CONFIDENCE
I CAN
BEAUTY
HOPE

FUTURE

LIGHTNESS

STANDING TALL

LAUGHTER

STRENGTH

ENERGY

MADE WHOLE

SMILES

POSITIVITY

ENDURANCE

BLESSED

TRUST

DANCING

REJOICING

SINGING

PROTECTED

ACCEPTED

FULLFILLED

It did not happen overnight, it took time for the Lord to heal me from the inside out, to teach me His ways, and I continue to learn day by day, how to stay in that rest and be joyful and have a peace. I can now say that these words relate closer to what I experience at present and I choose to stay in that place.

Fear, if left unchecked, will change you, it will change your life and it will change others' lives around you. I share later on in this book how this happened in my life.

I want you to recognise that spirit of the devil and RESIST it and be free from it BEFORE it becomes a problem AND ENSNARES YOU, changing you and others around you.

FEAR IF LEFT UNCHECKED WILL CHANGE YOU, IT WILL CHANGE YOUR LIFE AND IT WILL CHANGE OTHERS LIVES AROUND YOU.

Nip it in the bud BEFORE it bears fruit! Don't let it get a foothold in your life!

Submit yourselves therefore to God. Resist the devil, and he will flee from you.

James 4:7

SUBMIT TO GOD
RESIST THE devil

Submit means to yield to a superior force, resign or surrender to the power, will or authority of another.

Resist means to stand against, to withstand, to act in opposition, or to oppose, to fight against something or someone that is attacking you.

FEAR IS -

False Evidence Appearing Real!

I want to now share a story that shows this statement of fear being false evidence appearing real.

CHAPTER THREE

FALSE EVIDENCE APPEARING REAL

When I was a teenager, a friend and I were walking up an alleyway (through an old railway track) and it was dark. There were very few lights on, so it was hard to see clearly.

We saw something moving on one side. We stood and observed for a while, unsure of what it was, until our imaginations kicked in, and we thought it was someone standing in the shadows, who might want to harm us. We were afraid, and did not want to go up the alleyway. So we hovered about for a while unsure of what to do. We were undecided, on whether to chance it by running up the alleyway or go another way, which would take longer to where we wanted to go to.

We saw a police man who was walking close by, and we went to him in our nervously heightened teenager voices, telling him what we thought we saw in the alleyway. He went closer to investigate, as we cowered at a distance away behind him. He came back to us with a smile of amusement on his face. It turned out to be a bag blowing in the wind that had caught on some branches. You see the light was dim, all we could see was something moving in the shadows.

This may bring a smile to your face, but at that time it was very real to us, we were afraid! This was a good case of FEAR - **F**alse **E**vidence **A**ppearing **R**eal!

Even though he told us what it was, we asked him to walk behind us up the dark alleyway, just in case. That fear was there. Even after that night every time I walked up that way I still felt that fear and nearly ran up that alleyway, looking behind myself to see if anyone was following.

This is just a story of how subtle fear can be. A seed was sown that night and I was reminded of it every time I went to walk up that alleyway.

FEAR CAN BE SUBTLE!

CHAPTER FOUR

ABUSED BY MY FATHER

As I shared in the Introduction of this book when it all began. My life changed, at around 11-13 years of age.

The safe place, the place that I called home, was not safe anymore, living everyday not knowing what was going to happen. I avoided being alone with my father and would go out just to feel safe for a time, hoping that on my return someone else would be in the house. All of this was kept as a secret deep within me.

I started to read books until late at night, even on school nights, because I was unable to sleep until I heard my father come up the stairs and go to bed. I was always listening, always waiting and looking at the door handle of my bedroom door to see if he was coming in.

Then when my bedroom was changed around and my wardrobe was closer to the door, I started to push the wardrobe in front my door so that it could not be opened. I would watch the door and see the handle go down, but was relieved, that with the wardrobe in front of the door, my father could not come into the bedroom. Even though I had that security at night, when I pushed the wardrobe in front of the door, I could not sleep until I heard him go to bed.

You may ask, 'Where was my mother'? My mother worked a number of evenings and was not home until late, after everyone was in bed. She had no idea this was happening until I gave her the note.

I lived in fear,
- fear that I would be alone with him,
- fear that I would not be able to escape,
- fear of what he would do to me,
– fear of going to sleep at night,
– fear of speaking out and breaking up the family.

My father had said to me that if I told anyone what he was doing, that it would be my fault that the family would break up!!! Manipulation and fear.

As a child that was very real, so any despair I was feeling, I had to keep it hidden. As a young adolescent having to carry that burden, I had to hide what was going on, wanting to cry out but unable to because of fear, always watching, making sure that I was not left alone with my father and planning ways of escape.

I became aware that he was planning ways of being alone with me, for example, asking me to go for a drive with him or going out to the caravan that was parked in the driveway to help him sort out boxes. I soon learned that his intentions were not good ones.

When our caravan was at a caravan park, we were all going to go stay there one weekend. I must have been older and mature enough to stay alone and decided that I did not want to go, that I would stay at home. So the rest of my family left and I was in the house alone.

As the day went on, and I was in the house alone, I heard, 'He's coming back', I heard this so very clearly, that I have never forgotten it thirty plus years later. I kept hearing those words 'He's coming back, he's coming back'. I now know it was the Lord warning me, I did not know it at that time, but I know it now. I felt that urgency and I called a friend and asked if she could stay over with me. She was allowed to stay, which I also know was the Lord helping me.

My father did come back, I don't know what reason he gave to go home again, but his intentions were not good. My father would have had freedom to do what he wanted with no interruptions, knowing that my mother would not be back for a couple of days.

I thank the Lord that He warned me and I heard Him, and I took action that weekend.

One afternoon my father was coming at me in the kitchen, trying to touch me, I tried to hit him, but he ducked and found it quite amusing that I missed him. I ran to get away and ended up on the stairs leading to the bedrooms. I remember stopping on the stairs half way, thinking that this was not a good idea, so I pushed past him down the stairs again and out the back door.

My friend was just coming into my driveway, to call for me to go to the shop, that we both worked for, delivering papers. This was the time that I broke down with my friend and shared what was happening.

Was it during these years of abuse that the spirit of fear got a hold of me? I don't know. But for sure there were more seeds of fear sown as well as other seeds, of anger, bitterness, betrayal, self hatred and shame, etc.

When the abuse was heard about in school and in the village were we lived, that's when I felt shame. I knew people knew our business on the street where we lived, and in the shops that we shopped in and worked in. At that time, abuse was not spoken off so openly, it was usually dealt with behind closed doors.

At school, I had to hand my teacher a note telling him about the abuse. It was so humiliating, to be looked at differently, to be looked at as a child who has been abused.

Then on top of this, getting an internal examination by a doctor, taken to a police station to give a statement, and then being removed from my home to a children's home for a couple of weeks for safety.

My whole world was turned upside down. My family was divided. My life changed once again.

My family did split up, but it was not because of me speaking out, it was because of what my father did.

CHAPTER FIVE

LIVING WITH FEAR

I want to share some of the events in my life (this was over a number of years) when fear controlled and ensnared me and how my body reacted. You may witness to some of these things in your own life or have seen it in someone else's life.

I planned the times I would go to shop for food. Usually early first thing in the morning or last thing at night at the quietest times because when I went to a shop, I felt people where looking at me and could see the torment that I was in and I felt ashamed. Noise and crowds were also difficult. If there were too many people I would feel panic growing in me and noise seemed to be magnified and I would feel overwhelmed.

I would only do things that I was familiar and comfortable with, anything outside of that brought anxiety and panic.

I refused to go places when invited. I could not even go to a chippy and sit in and eat a meal, my family had to bring a carry-out home for me. People stopped asking me to go places, after a while, because they were so used to me refusing to go. This then had a counter attack, because I felt rejected, frustrated, ashamed, weak and I felt all the more lonely. Separated from others. I wanted to let people in, I wanted to 'be normal', I wanted acceptance and understanding, but did not even know how to begin to share what I was going through. I felt pathetic and worthless.

When I was receiving counselling, my counsellor had to visit with me at my home where I was most comfortable, because I could not go to them, even though they were based only a few miles away in a town that I knew well.

If I did go out in the evening, to a party or pub, I always had to have a number of drinks at home before venturing out to give me some confidence because I felt out of place and uncomfortable without that "dutch courage". It also helped loosen my tongue to talk to people. I usually ended up in tears, telling people my story in my drunken state.

Work was okay because it was at a private house and I did not see too many people there. After work I would just go to bed, I had no hope, I was lonely, I was depressed, I was in a very dark hole. Darkness seemed to surround me, I was burdened and could not see a way of escape out of that hole and the nightmare I was living in.

My husband and I had not planned a honeymoon (we were not long married), so when a couple of people pulled out of a skiing holiday and we were asked if we would like to go and fill their spaces we decided to go. It was a very spur of the moment decision, I did not have much time to think too much about it. When we were at the airport FEAR and ANXIETY was having such an effect on me that I was in the toilets throwing up and having diarrhoea. I nearly did not get on that plane. I actually said to my husband "I can't go. I can't do this".

At the hotel in Italy, the large group we were with all ate together in the hotel's restaurant. Most nights I could not go and eat with everyone else, I was unable to mix with people and felt very anxious. The noise level I could not tolerate, it seemed to be magnified and caused the anxiety to get stronger. When in that anxious state nausea would set in, so my appetite was suppressed. To my recollection I asked my husband to bring me up a crusty roll with butter and jam on those nights that I could not eat with the group. On the final days nearing the end of our holiday, I was able to eat with the rest of the group. On that occasion they were giving out gifts to some of the group. My husband was one of them.

They gave him a gift because he had looked after me so well, which was not untrue. He did take me into consideration throughout the holiday and I am so thankful for that. He did tend to all of my needs without one word of complaint.

Fear and anxiety affected my husband's holiday, our honeymoon, but it also instilled more shame of who I was and had become, how weak I felt amongst these strangers that seemed to do life so well. For many, many years after this, I would not fly, I would not go anywhere on a plane. Just like the time going up the alleyway, the thought of flying brought back that fear and nausea.

Trying to climb a wave breaker at the beach - my body froze I could not move. I did not feel fear even come on me but my body reacted. I needed my husband to get behind me and push me up.

When we went to a hotel and had a lovely room, I could not stay and we had to return home - ANXIETY and FEAR - again affecting others around me.

I became a bit stronger over time and was able to go out a bit more. I would plan my escape route, for example, if I was say at a meeting, for example I would sit at the back near the exit doors. I would carry pills to take and water to sip on if I needed them.

This was the lifestyle that I lived. Fear controlled what I did and how I felt. I bowed down to that fear and let it ensnare me. I hated who I was, who I had become, I felt weak. I hated how people looked at me in pity or in judgment for they did not see the battle going on in my head. They did not see the struggle, they did not see the dark place I was in, that even to go out was actually a step forward. When people have not experienced this mental struggle it can be hard for them to have compassion on those who are in that battle.

Fear can hide for a while and life can become easier, then it raises its ugly head again when maybe a stressful situation or circumstance happens. You don't even know that you are going through it until your body starts to react and your mind starts telling you that you can't do that and you start feeling sick or you are losing sleep, and you feel that fear again.

The first time I remember when I experienced fear, anxiety and depression was when I was living on my own in my twenties. I had a severe kidney infection that was not diagnosed for some time. I felt like I had a hang over all the time. My body became weaker and weaker and I could not eat or go anywhere. This sickness had a negative effect on my mental health and caused me to withdraw even more into myself. I felt a heaviness and depression upon me and was in a very dark place.

At that time I did not recognise or understand, that the torment that was going on inside of me from the abuse and from my past was having an effect on my body. My body was in dis-ease. At that time I was very bitter towards my father. I would have said back then that I would spit on his grave. That's how angry and bitter I had become towards him. It was like I was spitting venom.

When I shared with my doctor about the abuse she referred me to a counselling group for people that had been abused. What I remember about this group was that there were people of all ages still dealing with abuse from their childhood, but I think the most important thing I took from that group was I was not alone. For a long time I had felt alone, dealing with the torment and replays that nobody could understand, but that group told me that there were many others who were going through similar issues to mine.

The second time was just before I was getting married. A major change was happening in my life, outside of getting married, that caused a lot of extra work and stress. I was experiencing anxiety, sickness in my stomach, and palpitations. If I was not working, I was preparing for my wedding, running to shops, ordering items and planning etc. All the work and stress had once again brought fear and anxiety back to the surface. My body was in disease once again.

On my wedding day at the reception, I could feel that anxiety in my stomach, I did not eat much and coped the best I could. I escaped to our guest room when I felt overcome, trying to calm myself down again to go spend more time with the guests.

The next morning at the wedding breakfast with a few friends from the reception I felt that anxiety come on me and I quickly went to the bathroom before I burst into tears. Oh how I hated myself, hated how weak I felt, hated that I was not able to control those emotions.

I was very reserved around people or withdrawn would maybe be the better word. I did a lot of deep thinking in my head, but did not speak very much. Even as a teenager I struggled to even make eye contact with people. A friend tried to help me in this area, for she noticed when I was talking to her that I was looking at the wall and not at her, so she tried to help me, tried to encourage me to make eye contact. I found making eye contact with people, friends or strangers to be very uncomfortable. It took many years to overcome this.

Often when I was out with friends I heard 'does you friend not speak?' or 'your friend does not say a lot?'. I was "the friend". I found it very difficult to start up conversations, to talk with people. I felt uncomfortable. In my head I was talking, and sometimes when I did manage to speak, the words came out so quietly or out of tone that people did not hear me or I would have to repeat myself to be heard.

My first full time job was with quite a large group of ladies. I was so painfully quiet and withdrawn, I would have brought in a book and stuck my head in it over the lunch and tea breaks to help me get through those breaks and not have to make conversations with others.

This was how I lived. This was how fear and anxiety controlled my life. I was broken, tormented and ashamed.

CHAPTER SIX

WHEN MY BODY BROKE DOWN

After my wedding, the major change in my life that I have spoken of previously, separate to planning my wedding, was still ongoing. My workload was heavy, I worked very long hours to accomplish what needed to be done in order to keep on top of things, taking work home with me and working in the evenings, early starts, late finishing etc.

Then one evening my body broke down, it could not keep going, it could not withstand the pressure I was putting it under, I had a nervous breakdown.

This was something worse than I had ever felt before. It was a combination of stress, fear & anxiety that caused my body to start to shut down.

I remember that it was in the moment I allowed myself to rest that my body crashed. I allowed myself to sit down and watch a movie. I remember it was just that one thought that I could relax for a moment and watch a movie with my husband and nephew, as I recall.

The fear, stress and anxiety that had built up over a number of years had taken its toll on my body. You see it was never dealt with, that ROOT OF FEAR, so each time I was in stressful times, it just added to what was already there. My body could not take anymore. All the pent up anger and bitterness that I was holding onto towards my father and others was mixed in amongst that fear and stress.

My nervous system was affected. My body was in constant tension. I could not straighten my body out when lying in bed, I had to sleep with my legs curved, in a fatal position. I could hardly eat for about six weeks. I did not sleep well. Even the soles of my feet were sore, walking on them barefoot was uncomfortable. The fear was heightened even more. Those small things that I could do, like running my nephew to school or being left alone when my husband went to work, I struggled with. The daily things that I did that once was comfortable had become uncomfortable. My nerves would be jittering and jumpy especially first thing in the morning. I did not like the mornings because that was when I seemed to feel most anxious. I felt CONSTANT nausea in my stomach. There was a battle going on in my mind continually.

THE DAILY THINGS THAT I DID THAT ONCE WAS COMFORTABLE HAD BECOME UNCOMFORTABLE

FEAR - It had to start somewhere. Like everything else, every addiction, it had to start somewhere. Small to start with, but as more seeds are sown the stronger it becomes. Then strongholds, mindsets and wrong thinking begin to become established in the mind.

These next chapters of this book will explain how I became free from the spirit of fear.

CHAPTER SEVEN

THEN I MET JESUS

Therefore if any man be in Christ, he is a new creature: old things are passed away; behold, all things are become new.

2 Corinthians 5:17

I gave my life to the Lord on 13th April 2008. Saying a simple prayer asking Him to forgive me and to come into my life. I said to my husband that I wanted to go to church that evening, and at the end of the service the Pastor asked if anyone wanted to give their life to the Lord, and if they did to say this prayer of Salvation after him (Similar to the prayer I have given at the end of this book). I said this prayer to

God, from my heart, knowing that I wanted change, I had tried so long to hold everything together in my own strength, and could not do it anymore. So I made that commitment to God that evening, not really knowing or understanding what I was committing too. I also remember feeling a little fearful at the time as I said that prayer, because of the uncertainty of what was to come next.

When my husband and I returned home I shared with my husband that I had said the prayer and had given my life to the Lord. My husband was already a child of God.

I did not feel much different after asking Jesus to come into my life, but I did feel an excitement of what was to come. I wanted to know more about Jesus.

I GAVE MY LIFE TO JESUS AND BECAME A BORN AGAIN CHRISTIAN

The first thing, after only a few months on my walk with Jesus, He told me to forgive my mother, not my father, but my mother. He did this very directly, that I could not misunderstand Him.

My husband, my friend and I went to a meeting in a large agricultural shed to hear a man of God speak. We were sitting to the side of the stage close to the stage. The man was speaking and suddenly, just out of nowhere, in the middle of his message, turned directly to me and pointed directly at me and said to me "FORGIVE your mother!", he said it twice and that I was to forgive her right away, that it did not matter what she had done, but to FORGIVE HER. My friend grabbed my hand and squeezed it, this was without a doubt the Lord speaking to me through this man of God.

There had been some conflict and strife in my family which had taken its toll on me, I had become angry and bitter towards my mother. I don't say this to point any fingers, we all had a part to play, I had allowed unforgiveness to come into my heart. So God told me to FORGIVE. This was the start of my journey of healing.

FORGIVING MY MOTHER WAS THE START OF MY JOURNEY OF HEALING

I cried a lot in the first couple of years when I was alone with Jesus and with others, but they were tears of healing as the Lord started to heal me from the inside out, doing that deep work that only He can do. Forgiving my father, forgiving my mother, forgiving others and forgiving myself... It all started with forgiveness.

IT ALL STARTED WITH FORGIVENESS

I told the Lord I wanted to forgive my father even though my emotions were still screaming at me to hate him. I knew I had to forgive him so that the Lord could heal those deep wounds that only He could reach. I started to tell the Lord that I choose to forgive my father, that I was willing to forgive and asked the Lord to help me.

As time went on, I knew I had forgiven my father, or should I say "this was what I thought." I thought I had forgiven him because I did not feel that bitterness and anger rising up towards him anymore.

My husband and I go to events and shows putting up a pop up shop to sell products. We were setting up when we looked across the field and saw from a distant that my father was also a trader setting up his stand. My husband had come across my father at a show before, when I was not with him so recognised his stand.

Earlier, when we were queuing to be let into the field to set up, I could feel in my Spirit that something was not right, I was not able to put my finger on it, but I was feeling a sense of fear and anxiety, but had no reason to feel this way because I had traded at this show before, and was familiar with its set up. When I saw my father from a distance I knew this was what was causing the feeling that something was not right.

I had not seen or spoken to my father in 20-30 years. (I had moved and lived more that 50 miles away from our family home).

Knowing that my father was so close by set my emotions on a roller coaster. I prayed and talked to God, one minute I felt strong and the next I felt weak. I toyed with the idea to go and speak to him but could not bring myself to do it and did not feel led by the Lord to do it either. We finished the show and went home. I recognised that I still had some work to do with the Lord on this matter. There was a deeper work to be done in me, that I did not know was there.

Let all bitterness, and wrath, and anger, and clamour, and evil speaking, be put away from you, with all malice:

Ephesians 4:31

For if ye forgive men their trespasses, your heavenly Father will also forgive you. *Matthew 6:14*

Judge not, and ye shall not be judged: condemn not, and ye shall not be condemned: forgive, and ye shall be forgiven.

Luke 6:37

And when ye stand praying, forgive, if ye have ought against any: that your Father also which is in heaven may forgive you your trespasses *Mark 11:25*

CHAPTER EIGHT

FREEDOM FROM FEAR

The first thing I wanted the Lord to deal with was the fear; the fear that I was dealing with everyday. I wanted Jesus to deliver me from that FEAR, to touch me and take it all away. He can do this, He can do anything, nothing is impossible for God, but for me it was a "working through". He took me step by step, one day at a time, one obstacle at a time, one emotion at a time.

For with God nothing shall be impossible.
Luke 1:37

When I first started to go to church every week, I would open my mouth to sing the words of the songs but nothing much came out. I was not used to singing, so it took a while for that noise to start to come up and out of my mouth. As I continued to go to church, my voice became stronger and on this one occasion I was singing out loud, enjoying the songs we were singing, I remember thinking to myself that I was really enjoying praising and worshipping the Lord.

As I was standing singing, I felt an ache, a pain in my lower back and had to sit down. I lost all energy in my arms and felt sick. That day, as I sang to the Lord praising and worshipping Him, I was delivered from an evil spirit, right where I was sitting.

Another time I went to the church prayer meeting and went up for prayer. The elders laid hands on me and prayed as the Holy Spirit led them. I sat down after the prayer to the side of the room. I was in such a place of peace. How I would describe it was that I was in a beautiful garden or field and I was swinging on a swing that was attached to a beautiful big oak tree, kicking my legs out, with the sunshine on my face. It brought such a wonderful calm to me, I did not want to leave that place of peace.

These are two occasions that I remember, one of deliverance and one of great peace.

The Lord delivered me from that spirit of fear, BUT I was still fearful!

Why was I still fearful you may ask, if I had been delivered from the spirit of fear?

I had lived with fear for many years, so my mind had a pattern of thinking. I had listened to fear tell me I was weak, that I could not go out, that I could not go out to places where there were crowds of people. Fear would have said to me, "What if you pass out? What if you have a panic attack? What if you make a fool of yourself in front of people?" That's what I would have been hearing.

My confession also needed to change, I was speaking what I was feeling and hearing in my head. I was confessing death instead of life. I was still thinking and confessing as the old me, the person that was ensnared by fear. That was the old me, before I gave my life to the Lord and was born again.

Death and life are in the power of the tongue: and they that love it shall eat the fruit thereof.

Proverbs 18:21

Out of the same mouth proceeded blessing and cursing, My brethren, these things ought not so to be.

James 3:10

Pleasant words are as an honeycomb, sweet to the soul, and health to the bones.

Proverbs 16:24

I had learned bad habits. There were strongholds and beliefs in my mind, that had to be dealt with and changed.

My Spirit had been made alive when I asked Jesus into my life, being born again, but my soul needed some work, which is the mind, will and emotions. My confession needed to change and what I believed needed to change. What I meditated and listened and watched needed to change.

As a young Christian I had to be re-trained, with the Holy Spirit as my teacher. I did this by looking for scriptures on fear, I also spent time going for walks and talking with the Lord, giving Him my burdens and asking for His help. I was not alone anymore, for he never leaves us or forsakes us. I had the Lord to help me, to show me, to

TEACH ME HIS WAYS, which are better than mine.

For my thoughts are not your thoughts, neither are your ways my ways, saith the Lord. For as the heavens are higher than the earth, so are my ways higher than your ways, and my thoughts than your thoughts.

Isaiah 55:8-9

I started by meditating on the Word of God.

Meditation means the turning or revolving of a subject in the mind; serious contemplation.

Let the words of my mouth, and the meditation of my heart, be acceptable in thy sight, O Lord, my strength, and my redeemer.

Psalm 19:14

What it took was a RENEWING of my MIND. That's where it started, so that's where it had to get sorted.

CHAPTER NINE

RENEWING OF THE MIND

You may ask, "How do you renew your mind?"

The answer is, "In the word of God".

- I confessed the word
- I meditated on the word
- I listened to the word and listened to teachers and preachers
- I did things afraid
- I self talked, replacing the 'I can't' with 'I can' with the Lord's help.

These are some of the scriptures I confessed and meditated on. Especially last thing at night and first thing in the morning. My body would have been tense at night when I was laying in bed trying to get over to sleep, I would have meditated on the word until my body relaxed and sleep came. I kept them in my mind, repeating them over and over, breaking the words down until peace came and I fell asleep.

For God hath not given us the spirit of fear; but of power, and of love, and of a sound mind.

2 Timothy 1:7

No weapon that is formed against thee shall prosper; and every tongue that shall rise against thee in judgment thou shalt condemn. This is the heritage of the servants of the Lord, and their righteousness is of me, saith the Lord.

Isaiah 54:17

God is my strength and power: and he maketh my way perfect.

2 Samuel 22:33

I can do all things through Christ which strengtheneth me.

Philippians 4:13

Nay, in all these things we are more than conquerors through him that loved us.

Romans 8:37

What shall we then say to these things? If God be for us, who can be against us?
Romans 8:31

In God have I put my trust: I will not be afraid what man can do unto me.
Psalms 56:11

Ye are of God, little children, and have overcome them: because greater is he that is in you, than he that is in the world.
1 John 4:4

I made the scripture personal and confessed them out of my mouth, over myself ie God you are MY strength and power: you make MY way perfect. I can do all things through Christ who strengthens me.

CONFESS
MEDITATE
PERSONALISE

When reading the Word this scripture really jumped out at me, and I grabbed a hold of it.

Take therefore no thought for the morrow: for the morrow shall take thought for the things of itself. Sufficient unto the day is the evil thereof.

Matthew 6:34

Fear is also worrying about tomorrow. The Lord would have reminded me of this scripture regularly, when I felt myself start to think upon the next day, for example, if I was having a meeting and I was not looking forward to it, I would be reminded about not giving that meeting any thought until the next day came. This really did help me put things into perspective.

I have shared my testimony of how fear got a hold of me and what my life was like. How that stinking spirit of fear had enslaved me.

I have also shared how I became free of fear, by giving my life to God, by confession, meditation and the renewing of my mind by reading and hearing the word of God.

I am now FREE FROM FEAR, that debilitating spirit that ensnares and enslaves. It's not to say I don't sense or feel fear at times, but now when I recognise it, I can say.

"NO DEVIL, you are not welcome here. BE GONE IN JESUS NAME. I have power, love and a sound mind. I FEAR NOT. I can do all things through Christ who strengthens me!"

Submit yourselves therefore to God. Resist the devil, and he will flee from you.
James 4:7

So ye have not received the spirit of bondage again to fear, but ye have received the Spirit of adoption, whereby we cry, Abba Father. *Romans 8:15*

I say to you today don't let fear get a hold of your life - KICK IT OUT!

Remember it has to start somewhere, by one wee thought, - anything that steals your peace, Kick it out!

Start to challenge those thoughts. If you are feeling anxious, look at what you are thinking about, who you have been listening to. Did you spend time with someone who was fearful?

If this happens go to the Word, talk to God, cast your burdens onto Him and repent. Get rid of that fear and anxiety. Don't let it linger, treat it like a bad smell, throw it out, put it under your feet where it belongs.

The Word says if you keep company with the wrong people that you can become like them.

Make no friendship with an angry man; and with a furious man thou shalt not go: Lest thou learn his ways, and get a snare to thy soul.

Proverbs 22:24-25

It is so important to have some people in your life that are like minded. Who love the Lord and who will not judge you for where you are, but will love you and support you as you grow in the Lord Jesus Christ.

FEAR comes by <u>hearing and believing</u> the LIES of the enemy.

THE DEVIL IS A LIAR!

Find out the truth by going to the Word. If it does not line up with the Word of God then Kick it out! The devil is a liar!

John 8:44 ...He was a murderer from the beginning, and abode not in the truth, because there is no truth in him. When he speaketh a lie, he speaketh of his own: for he is a liar, and the father of it.

One of the first things the Lord had me do was to confess over myself 'I have a strong immune system'. Life and death are in the power of the tongue, I was speaking life over my body.

When I was walking, I confessed those words over myself. 'I have a strong immune system, by Jesus stripes I am healed.'. You see that continual fear, stress and anxiety had taken a toll on my body. I did not know it myself but the Lord knew it.

Who his own self bare our sins in his own body on the tree, that we, being dead to sins, should live unto righteousness: by whose stripes ye were healed. 1 Peter 2:24 (also Isaiah 53:5)

WE HAVE TO DO SOMETHING, WE HAVE TO TAKE ACTION, when the Lord tells us to do something WE MUST DO IT! HE KNOWS BETTER.

For my thoughts are not your thoughts, neither are your ways my ways, saith the Lord. For as the heavens are higher than the earth, so are my ways higher than your ways, and my thoughts than your thoughts.

Isaiah 55:8-9

CHAPTER TEN

MINDLESSNESS

Most of us I'm sure, have sometimes eaten mindlessly.

Eating while watching something on television, is one definite way of doing this. I know there have been times when I was so focused on a programme that I could have eaten half a large bar of chocolate before I even realised it. I was not focused on what I was eating or how much I ate, I just ate mindlessly. Then maybe 15 mins later I know I have eaten too much and I felt uncomfortable or felt a bit sick because of too much sugar. My thoughts were not mindful, my focus was on something else, the television programme.

Have you ever been listening to someone talk, then your mind wanders off and you are thinking about something else? The person you are listening to still thinks you are hearing what they are saying because you are maybe nodding in all the right places. Then that person asks you a question and you have to admit that your mind wandered and could they repeat what they had been sharing or asking you. This is the same as mindless eating, your mind is not focused on what you are eating or hearing because you have lost your focus. Your mind has been <u>mindless</u> instead of <u>mindful</u>.

Don't let your MIND WANDER to whatever it wants.

Don't lose your FOCUS on what you are doing.

We can learn to discipline our thinking and watch over our thoughts just like we would a CHILD and CORRECT them when necessary.

DISCIPLINE YOUR THINKING

This is an area I am still working on, I am recognising and exercising my authority over my thinking and NOT BELIEVING EVERYTHING IT TELLS ME.

Think about it, what you FOCUS and MEDITATE on is what you will RECEIVE.

The word says to mediate on the word day and night.

This book of the law shall not depart out of thy mouth; but thou shalt meditate therein day and night, that thou mayest observe to do according to all that is written therein: for then thou shalt make thy way prosperous, and then thou shalt have good success.

Joshua 1:8

Finally, brethren, whatsoever things are true, whatsoever things are honest, whatsoever things are just, whatsoever things are pure, whatsoever things are lovely, whatsoever things are of good report; if there be any virtue, and if there be any praise, thing on these things.

Philippians 4:8

Think about this - What if you meditated on these words:-

Greater is he that is in me than he that is in the world.

1 John 4:4

I am full of power, of the Spirit of the Lord, and of justice and might.

Micah 3:8

How would you feel?

The Word sets us free, it gives us power, revelation, understanding, wisdom, direction, knowledge, it tells us what the Will of God is and it gives us answers to our problems.

In the beginning was the Word, and the Word was with God, and the Word was God.

John 1:1

Can you imagine if your mind was so focused and steadfast on the Word, on Jesus what you would be?

CHAPTER ELEVEN

WHAT I FEARED CAME UPON ME

For the thing which I greatly feared is come upon me, and that which I was afraid of is come unto me.

Job 3:25

Job recognised that he had received what he was thinking about, what he feared happened. He received what he had feared.

This happened to me on this one occasion that I remember distinctly. I was fearful of cutting myself on a tin, every time I opened a tin of dog food, that thought came into my head. 'You are going to cut yourself'. Then it did happen, I sliced my finger with a tin. So I received what I feared, what I had been thinking was going to happen. I had been allowing that thought to continually come into my mind every time I opened a tin. What I was afraid of came unto me!

I don't particularly like opening tins, because some of the lids do not pull off easily. I do not fear opening a tin now, but I am sensible and know my capabilities. If a lid does not pull of easily, instead of fighting with it and struggling with it I ask my husband to pull the rest of the lid off for me. You might smile at this but I am using wisdom.

My husband can look at something and figure out how it works just by looking at it,. He has great hands and can put them to most things. I on the other hand will turn it upside down, inside out and still not find out how it works.

On one occasion I ordered a tin of spice, it came in a lovely little red square tin with a strange lid, I looked and looked at the lid trying to figure out how to open it and was thinking I may need to use a tin opener somehow. I asked my husband could he see how to open it, at a glance he took a knife out the drawer and used its edge to leaver off the lid to reveal the spice.

This is why the Lord brought my husband and myself together! HA HA!
So I leave some things to my husband and focus on my own special gifts that the Lord has given me.

Going back to what we meditate on. If we meditate on fear, dread, worry about something, then that's what we are going to attract. In other words that's what we will receive, it will come upon us. It is so important that we understand this today. We need to take authority over our thinking.

I have never forgotten cutting my finger on that tin, it taught me a great lesson and when you find the scripture that applies in God's Word it shows you the power of meditation and the power of what we think and speak.

CHAPTER 12

THERE'S POWER IN THE WORD

HOW MUCH MORE POWERFUL would we be if we meditated on the Word of God! What would we receive?? Remember every promise in this book is ours!

Our minds are continually thinking about something, if it's not the Word of God then it is something else.

The Lord tells us in His word:-

Casting all your care upon him; for he cares for you.

1 Peter 5:7

Be careful for nothing; but in everything by prayer and supplication with thanksgiving let your requests be made known unto God. And the peace of God, which passeth all understanding, shall keep your hearts and minds through Christ Jesus.
Philippians 4:6-7

When we give over all our cares to the Lord and make known our requests to Him we can have the peace of God which will keep our hearts and minds.

I have grown in this area, many times I tried to carry everything in life myself, I have tried to work it all out, I have worked harder when finances where tight, I have tried new ventures and they have failed, I have done things on my own strength without consulting the Lord. Doing it on my own strength was exhausting, I worried, I carried the burden myself, I felt weighed down.

Come unto me, all ye that labour and are heavy laden, and I will give you rest. Take my yoke upon you, and learn of me; for I am meek and lowly in heart: and ye shall find rest unto your souls. For my yoke is easy, and my burden is light.

Matthew 11:28-30

When things were difficult financially in our business, or we were short staffed, my husband and I seemed to work all the harder, doing small shows just to sell the stock that we had, working six days a week, taking whatever work came in to help the cash flow in the business. We were both tired and stressed. We were so tired sometimes that instead of eating, we lay down because our bodies needed rest more than food at that moment. Our time with the Lord grew shorter and shorter. Our focus was to work, to keep the cashflow coming in, and to meet the deadlines for the orders that had been received.

Outside of the business we were managing two houses, and two gardens etc. Any time we were not working we would have been maintaining two properties.

While I was gardening, the second garden that week, I hurt my lower back. This was because of the stress and tension I had been putting myself under. I was overworked, tired, stressed, anxious and worried.

I had also stopped going to the prayer meeting at church, 'I was too tired' I had told myself.

Pulling away from the Lord did not help our situation but made our situation worse.

The damage I had done to my back made it all the more difficult. I could not drive because of the pain down my leg, I could not even lift my right leg into the car, I had to pull my leg up with my hands.

At church on that Sunday of that week, I went up for prayer. I just about made it to church, even though the pain was difficult to bear to the extent that I had to go to the bathroom and gag as I thought I was going to throw up with the pain. The Lord touched me and I found relief from the pain, the pain left. Over the following days my back became stronger and stronger. I praise God for healing me!

Through all of that experience, I have learned now to first go to the Lord, not pull away from Him, but to do the opposite and draw closer to Him.

When we are at rest, and live in the peace of God, we are in a position to easily hear His voice.

IN TIMES OF STRUGGLE DRAW EVEN CLOSER TO GOD

Another area I am growing in is to go to God in FAITH, so that my prayers to Him are FAITH FILLED and not FEAR FILLED.

Where does faith come from - faith comes by hearing and hearing the Word of God.

So then faith cometh by hearing, and hearing by the word of God.
Romans 10:17

But let him ask in FAITH, nothing wavering. For he that wavers is like a wave of the sea driven with the wind and tossed. For let not that man think that he shall receive any thing of the Lord.
James 1:6-7

I have also noticed on my journey with the Lord that I hear Him more clearly, when I am at peace, I am able to receive direction and answers. When I have been tormented, fearful and anxious I would have become frustrated, because I was not hearing which way to go, there was too much noise going on in my head to hear what the Lord was saying to me.

I sought the Lord, and he answered me; he delivered me from all my fears.
Psalm 34:4

Listen to yourself.
Hear yourself.
Whats coming our of you mouth?
Are you talking faith or are you talking fear?

Are you speaking blessings or are you speaking curses?

Are you speaking with power and might or are you speaking in defeat?

But those things which proceed out of the mouth come forth from the heart; and they defile the man.

Matthew 15:18

IF YOU HEAR YOURSELF SPEAKING FEARFUL WORDS, THEN THAT'S WHAT'S IN YOUR HEART.

Death and life are in the power of the tongue: and they that love it shall eat the fruit thereof.

Proverbs 18:21

DEATH AND LIFE - WHICH ONE ARE YOU SPEAKING?

Out of the same mouth proceeded blessing and cursing. My brethren, these things ought not so to be.

James 3:10

DO YOU REALLY BELIEVE GODS WRITTEN WORD?

ARE YOU DOING WHAT IS WRITTEN?

FOR IT SAYS 'FEAR NOT' MANY TIMES IN THE WORD.

If we are in fear then, we are not believing, WE ARE NOT IN FAITH. Fear and faith cannot be operating together, at the same time.

Have you ever tried laughing and being angry at the same time? Have you ever been annoyed with someone and they start to make you laugh. There's a bit of resistance to start with but you cannot laugh and be angry or annoyed at the same time. Think about it!

Doth a fountain send forth at the same place sweet water and bitter?

James 3:11

REFRESH your memory on the stories of the bible, WHAT GOD DID for His children - he split the red sea, closed the lions mouths, they came out unharmed from the fiery furnace, HE created Heaven and earth! Encourage yourself in the Lord.

And David was greatly distressed; for the people spake of stoning him, because the soul of all the people was grieved, every man for his sons and for his daughters: but David encouraged himself in the Lord his God.

1 Samuel 30:6

It says He's the same yesterday, today and forever, that He is no respecter of persons.

Jesus Christ the same yesterday, and today, and forever.

Hebrews 13:8

DO YOU TRUST GOD, YOUR FATHER IN HEAVEN?

DO YOU BELIEVE THAT HE LOVES YOU AND WILL PROTECT YOU, and that He can do anything even when it looks impossible?

But Jesus beheld them, and said unto them, With men this is impossible; but with God all things are possible.
Matthew 19:26

When a young child comes to you in tears because something has frightened them or they are hurt. What do you do? You might wrap your arms around them and hold them until that fear goes and they feel protected and safe. Then you may reassure them they are going to be okay, and you might kiss it better or kiss them. The child goes skipping away because they know Father's got this. Childlike faith!

In the older children, you may comfort them first or speak to them, you might encourage them with your words, or tell them "you can do this", or "this is what you need to do", with the wisdom and knowledge that you have.

Learn to REST in the Lord. Take time out just for you and the Lord.

Rest in your FATHER'S ARMS, all he has to do is hold you and you will feel so much better, knowing that He will protect you.

The Lord is my strength and my shield; my heart trusted in him, and I am helped: therefore my heart greatly rejoiceth; and with my song will I praise him.

Psalm 28:7

If you can remember the three C's:-

Challenge that thought - recognise fear, worry, anxiety

Cast it out

Change that thought - with the truth of the Word of God.

Casting down imaginations, and every high thing that exalteth itself against the knowledge of God, and bringing into captivity every thought to the obedience of Christ;

2Cor 10: 5-7

Yes - renewing the mind takes effort - but what a freedom we can live in, what a peace we can experience. How wonderful it is to be able to rest in peace even in a storm, to have a joy even when things are difficult.

CHAPTER THIRTEEN

STRONGHOLDS

If you can think of these illustrations.

A paper bag that you would receive when you buy a card does its purpose, to keep a bunch of cards together and protect them, but it is not very strong. You could punch through it or tear it open quite easily.

This represents the odd thought of fear or doubt. All you would need to do is say NO I am not going to believe that. You can cast out that thought quite easily.

STRONGER BAG

Then we have the stronger bag made of strong cardboard that are made to carry a heavier weight, like the bags you would buy in the card shops for birthday or Christmas presents with a ribbon handle.

This represents you having more regular thoughts, feeling fearful, maybe losing sleep. This time it takes the sword, the word of God to get you free. Confession, and meditation.

BOXED PRISON CELL

Then we have a strong box, the lids or flaps are closed and you are in darkness, it will take time to find your way out to get free because of the strongholds and mindsets that you have and because of possible health issues.

You are now dealing with other issue's - not just fear.

THIS WAS WERE I WAS - BOXED IN - IN DARKNESS WITH HEALTH ISSUES

Disease is DIS - EASE in the body.

Thou wilt keep him in perfect peace, whose mind is stayed on thee: because he trusted in thee.

Isaiah 26:3

He shall not be afraid of evil tidings: his heart is fixed, trusting in the Lord. His heart is established, he shall not be afraid, until he see his desire upon his enemies.

Psalms 112:7-8

So that we may boldly say, The Lord is my helper, and I will not fear what man shall do unto me.

Hebrews 13:6

There is a battle going on RIGHT NOW. The devil is after your peace.

TAKE UP YOUR SWORD and fight the good fight of FAITH.

1 Tim 6:12

Psalm 56 is a powerful Psalm to confess and mediate on.

What time I am afraid, I will trust in thee. In God I will praise his word, in God I have put my trust; I will not fear what flesh can do unto me.

Psalm 56: 3-4

When I cry unto thee, then shall mine enemies turn back: this I know; for God is for me. In God will I praise his word: in the Lord will I praise his word. In God have I put my trust: I will not be afraid what man can do unto me.

Psalm 56: 9-11

YOU CAN DO THIS!

YOU HAVE LOVE, POWER AND A SOUND MIND IN CHRIST!

DON'T LISTEN TO THOSE LIES ANYMORE, REMEMBER satan is the father of lies.

FEAR is false evidence appearing real.

YOU ARE AN OVERCOMER, A CHILD OF GOD, STAND UP, STAND STRONG!

YOU ARE NOT ALONE - FOR GOD IS WITH YOU AND WILL NEVER LEAVE YOU OR FORSAKE YOU.

For whatsoever is born of God overcometh the world: and this is the victory that overcometh the world, even our faith. Who is he that overcometh the world, but he that believeth that Jesus is the Son of God?
1 John 5:4-5

Remember don't let those thoughts become strongholds in your mind.

FEAR IF LEFT UNCHECKED WILL CHANGE YOU, IT WILL CHANGE YOUR LIFE AND IT WILL CHANGE OTHER'S LIVES AROUND YOU.

LIVE LIFE TO THE FULLNESS WITH LOVE, JOY AND PEACE.

If the Son therefore shall make you free, ye shall be free indeed.

John 8:36

If you would like to ask the Lord into your life, at the end of this book you will find a short prayer of Salvation.

Remember, Jesus loves you - you are not alone!

ABOUT THE AUTHOR

I have been on an amazing journey with the Lord Jesus Christ. He has been transforming me from a broken, fearful and bitter person to a new person. I can now hold my head up high, I can make eye contact with others, I have boldness and confidence, I can love others and also receive love from others, I am free from the torment of my past and I have peace and joy in my heart. I am free from fear!

I give the Lord praise and thanks for the completion of this book and what He has done in my life.

I could not have written this book on my own. Never would I have even considered writing a book before I met the Lord.

I never knew love until I asked Jesus into my life. I had a void, an emptiness in my heart that could not be filled. Jesus was the one that has made me complete. I encourage you to ask Jesus into your life.

If you are in an abusive situation, or have been abused, I would encourage you to share with someone who you can trust, who will support you. So many are afraid to speak out because of fear, manipulation, shame, embarrassment and feelings of being a failure.

Please remember, it is not you that has done the wrong but the one that has abused you.

Jesus is the only one that can heal that deep pain and brokenness, deep within. All you have to do is to sincerely ask Him into your heart, He loves you and wants to help you. He is waiting on you to call on His name. He wants to have a relationship with you, to talk with you, to walk with you, to guide you, to heal you and most importantly to love you.

If you would like to ask the Lord into your life please pray the Prayer of Salvation which is at the back of this book.

For more information please contact Denise Montgomery at

Bridgeview Pentecostal Assembly,
104 Craigadick Road,
Maghera,
County Londonderry,
Northern Ireland,
BT46 5DH.

Email -
deepworksministry@gmail.com
Find out more at -
www.facebook.com/JesusSetsFree

PRAYER OF SALVATION

Heavenly Father,
Thank you for sending your Son, Jesus, to die for me. I believe that You raised him from the dead on the third day and that Jesus is alive today.

I repent of my sin and ask you to forgive me and make me brand new.

Come into my heart, Lord Jesus, and be my Saviour. By faith I receive your gift of salvation. I am ready to trust you as my Lord and Saviour. Fill me with your Holy Spirit.

You are the Lord of my life. I thank you that the old life is gone and a new life has begun, in Jesus name, Amen

If you prayed this prayer from your heart, you are now a born again Christian.

For by grace are ye saved through faith; and that not of yourselves: it is a gift of God (Eph 2:8-9).

This is the beginning of an amazing journey you are about to go on.

For I know the thoughts that I think toward you, saith the Lord, thoughts of peace, and not of evil, to give you an expected end.   Jeremiah 29:11

The thief cometh not, but for to steal, and to kill, and to destroy: I am come that they

might have life, and that they might have it more abundantly.

John 10:10

We would like to pray for you and help you take your next steps in Christ.

You can contact us by email:-

deepworksministry@gmail.com

or write to:-
Bridgeview Pentecostal Assembly,
104 Craigadick Road,
Maghera,
County Londonderry,
Northern Ireland
BT45 5DH

Printed in Great Britain
by Amazon